72 Hours in Vienna

A smart swift guide to delicious food, great rooms and what to do in Vienna, Austria.

TRIP PLANNER GUIDES

Copyright © 2016 Trip Planner Guides

All rights reserved. No part of this book may be reproduced in any form or by any electronic or mechanical means including information storage and retrieval systems – except in the case of brief quotations in articles or reviews – without the permission in writing from its publisher.

Although the author and publisher have made every effort to ensure that the information in this book was correct at press time, the author and publisher do not assume and hereby disclaim any liability to any party for any loss, damage, or disruption caused by errors or omissions, whether such errors or omissions result from negligence, accident, or any other cause.

ISBN-13: 978-1523315079

ISBN-10: 1523315075

TABLE OF CONTENTS

	Before You Get Started…	5
1	Welcome to Vienna	7
2	Overview of Vienna's Neighborhoods	22
3	How to Get Your Bearings and Avoid Getting Lost	28
4	Top 20 Attractions in Vienna	33
5	Daily Itinerary Planner & Day One	41
6	Day Two in Vienna	51
7	Day Three in Vienna	58
8	Viennese Cuisine	60
9	Dining in Vienna	67
10	Vienna by Night	71
11	Accommodation	74
12	Other Recommended Places to Visit	80
13	German Language Essentials	82

14 Conclusion   96

BEFORE YOU GET STARTED

We've put together a quick set of tips for maximizing the information provided in this guide.

Insider tips: Found in italics throughout the guide, these are golden nuggets of information picked up during our travels. Use these handy tips to save money, skip the queues and uncover hidden gems.

Maps: This guide connects you to the most up-to-date city and transport maps. Step-by-step instructions are included on how to access. We highly recommend reviewing these maps PRIOR to departing on your trip.

Itineraries: While we have enclosed memorable itineraries for your use, we understand that sometimes you just want to venture out on your own. That is why all major attractions, hotels, restaurants and entertainment venues are tagged with the neighborhood that houses them. In doing so, you'll know what's nearby when planning your adventures.

Budget: Prices at time of publication are provided for all major attractions and a pricing scale is provided for all hotels, restaurants and entertainment.

Websites: To ensure you have the most up-to-date information prior to departure we have included links to venue websites for your convenience. Simply enter the url into your favorite browser to load the webpage.

1 WELCOME TO VIENNA

Vienna is one of the most spellbinding cities you could ever have the privilege of visiting. Home of kings and queens, stupendous architecture and more artistic geniuses than any other country in Europe, it is a fascinating, vibrant and utterly rewarding holiday destination.

Renowned as the "Music Capital of the World", Vienna was the home of Mozart, Haydn, Beethoven, Schubert, Brahms, Bruckner, Mahler, Strauss, and many more revered composers. Vienna is also home to some of the world's greatest architectural masterpieces, including majestic Baroque castles and perfectly landscaped gardens. Sigmund Freud, the world's first psychoanalyst, was also born here. Also known as the City of Dreams, Vienna has inspired countless people through the centuries and nowadays, continues to overwhelm all who visit.

Today, stepping into Vienna is like taking a journey back in time; like being transported into another realm. You will see some of the most magnificent palaces and castles in Europe, many of which have now been converted to museums. The marvelous designs of these buildings feature undulating outlines using delicate colors and are richly-adorned with ornaments. You will see countless pillars and statues showcasing intricate details. Some say that compared to other major cities in the world, where buildings and edifices are just plain concrete and steel, Viennese walls seems to have a life of their own. The city breathes, pulsates and thrives as if playing a part in the modern Austrian's everyday existence.

In Vienna's countryside, you will find vast vineyards which grow and harvest some of the best grapes in the world. Thanks to a very favorable climate and rich soil, these grapes are turned into quality wines of distinctive taste, which are widely sought by discerning connoisseurs all over the world.

Vienna offers a mixture of everything, from interesting places to see, fun and unique activities to enjoy, and delectable meals to savor. The end result? Travelers never run out of choices!

A visit to Vienna will be a trip that will forever be etched in your memory, long after you've returned home, revisiting them again even just in your dreams. These lines may sound poetic, but that feeling within you will be ignited by the charm, the unique characteristics and the magic of this place. Vienna is, without a doubt, a city to remember. As the saying goes, "Music makes the world go round".

It does, and it all started here, in Vienna. So, take a 3-day journey to this magnificent city and come see for yourselves what others have admired for centuries.

A Brief Look Back in Time

Austria's crowning glory, Vienna is the center of cultural, economic and political affairs of the country. The city's roots trace back to Celtic and Roman settlements which were transformed into a Medieval and Baroque city and eventually became the capital of the Austro-Hungarian empires. The earliest recorded settlers of Vienna were the Celts in 500 BC. The Babenberg Dynasty expanded their rule to Vienna in 1145 making the city the center of their monarchy.

In 1440, the Habsburg dynasty came into being and took residency in Vienna. This has been the most powerful empire in Europe, one which ruled over Austria for many centuries. This great monarchy built their empire seat here, in Vienna, eventually expanding their regime over the neighboring European countries of Turkey, Italy, Netherlands and many more. This dynasty has made a remarkable impact in Vienna, and this is vividly shown through the number of brilliant architectural masterpieces sprawling throughout the city.

Vienna actually developed into a major city in the latter part of the 18th century. This is also the year when the famous Ringstrasse, the major boulevard that traverses the inner part of the city, was built. It was in 1919 when Vienna became the capital of the First Republic of Austria. Through the years, the city had continuous and fast development in the fields of architecture, music, education and the arts. In 1938, the Germans took over Vienna, and the city lost its status as a capital to Berlin. The city greatly suffered during the Second World War. Damage to infrastructure and loss of lives was severe. On April of 1945, Vienna and the whole of Austria were finally separated from Germany.

The years following the war proved to be very challenging for the Viennese. These were the years of uncertainty as the city was controlled by the Allied Commission (the four powers: USA, UK, France and the Soviet Union). This period lasted until the Austrian State Treaty was signed in May of 1955. It was during that year that Vienna came back to life. Reconstruction and restoration took place for the major structures and buildings in the city which were greatly damaged by the war. The State Opera and the Burgtheatre reopened to the public. The rest is history, so they say.

Today, Vienna bears very little signs of the struggles that she went through during those challenging years. In fact, in 2005, it ranked first in the Economist Intelligence Unit's survey as the "world's most livable city".

Today, Vienna is a hub for international conventions, and is one of the cities in Europe which attracts the most number of tourists per year.

What to Know Before You Go

Here are some key essentials to get you started on your Vienna vacation.

- **Learning a few key phrases in German** will help you break that initial contact with locals. Although Most Viennese, and many Austrians in general, speak English reasonably well, it's useful and courteous to know at least the basics like "Good morning/please/thank you/excuse me etc". Pick up an English/German pocket dictionary before you leave home, and make sure it includes a 'food section' to help you navigate restaurant menus.

- **Greet people as you enter a shop/bank.** It's the local thing to do and is one of the biggest differences between Europeans and Americans.

- Austria is in the Euro Zone and **the Euro is the country's only currency**. ATMs, known as *Bankomats* in this part of the world, are widely available, with pin-enabled credit cards accepted everywhere, except small markets. Do note that exchanging travelers' checks can be a difficult endeavor, so opt to go without if you can. Your cheapest option is to have a debit card which incurs no international withdrawal fees, use the ATM, and pay for everything in cash. Vienna, generally speaking, is a moderately expensive city to visit; slightly dearer than Munich but cheaper than Rome.

- If you want to call Austria, note that the **country code is 43, while Vienna's area code is 1**.

If your loved ones from the US are trying to get a hold of you in your hotel room, they will have to dial: 011 (US international code to dial out) + 43 (Austria's country code) + 1 (Vienna's area code) + phone number. Example: 011 43 1 1234567

- Here are some important **emergency numbers** to keep handy during your trip:

122 – Fire Brigade

144 – Ambulance

112 – Police

112 – General European emergency number (i.e. if you don't know what number to call)

- Most tourist sites are open daily, however note that **some museums are closed on Mondays or Tuesdays**. Before you head out, visit their websites to double check the hours. Normally, sites operate on a seasonal timetable, with longer hours in summer and shorter opening hours in winter. On Wednesdays, museums typically have longer operating hours (they may close 2 hours later than normal), which gives you extra time to sightsee for the day.

- **Working hours in Vienna are 9 am to 6 pm**, with retail outlets usually staying open until 8 pm and, in the case of supermarkets for example, even 10 pm. Vienna is still quite traditional, so after 6 pm on weekdays, and all day Sunday, you'll find very little open. Use this time to sightsee and enjoy the wonderful parks in the city.

- **Eating hours in Vienna are standard** – Your breakfast (if your hotel serves it) may be anytime between 6 am-10 am, lunch between 11 am – 2 pm, and dinner can be from 6 pm to as late as 10 pm. Note that some restaurants close anytime between 10 pm to midnight, so always check the restaurant first to make sure it's open.

- **Get high**! If you think Vienna is insanely beautiful at street level, wait until you see her from up high. The Ferris wheel at the Prater Amusement park is not only fun but also grants great city views. For a more encompassing vista, head up to Kahlenberg peak on a crystal clear day and you'll be gob smacked at just how stunning this whole region is.

- **Go to some effort to look the part**. Viennese are quite a dressy lot; in fact locals may seem much classier than even Parisians, at first glance. Although a good pair of comfy shoes are a must, picking a color *other* than sparkling white will help you blend in a little better.

- At the risk of sounding very Fawlty Towers-like, **never mention the war or make a Nazi joke**, in front of locals. New York may have a "Soup Nazi" thanks to *Seinfeld* but Viennese would be utterly appalled at the mere thought. This is a painful chapter of the country's history so do avoid it at all cost.

- Don't freak out should you walk into a restaurant and spot a dog sitting quietly under a table. Much like in Paris, **dogs are the norm here in Vienna** and are welcomed in many eating establishments. However, they are trained to be diffident of strangers so approaching to pet one, without asking the owner's permission, is certainly not recommended. Oh, and you'll also discover that smoking is still allowed in some parts of some restaurants, but these are usually secluded and easy enough to avoid if you wish.

- Something else to avoid, is dog poo. No matter how proper the Viennese may be, they're not in the habit of picking up their pooches' business and, considering there are so many dogs in the city, well…one plus one does equal two! **Watch your step**.

- Much like their German neighbors, Viennese may appear stand-offish at first, when in fact they are a very friendly lot once you get to know them. And share a few beers with them. **Respect people's personal space and try to not come across as too boisterous**.

- You may not see any turnstiles at train stations, yet do not take this to mean Viennese inspectors are slack about controls. They're not. **Always buy a ticket before boarding any type of public transport** or it will cost you dearly.

- **Littering is highly prohibited** here and fines are almost double what they are for free-riding on trains and buses.

- **Vienna boasts an amazing café scene** and this is so intrinsic to the local culture that it's even been inscribed as a UNESCO Intangible Heritage. Coffee is best savored slowly, outdoors, on a sunny day.

- Don't mind the nudity...the Viennese certainly don't! **Topless sunbathing is common** in Austria, so don't be shocked to see bare-chested women in parks and public swimming pools and spots along the river. It's perfectly normal here.

Climate & Best Time to Visit

Vienna has a continental climate with a large seasonal temperature variance. The heat of summer may reach up to a high of 25°C (77°F), while the colder months of winter can have the temperature dipping down to an average of -2°C (27°F). Spring and autumn are generally mild.

The best months to experience Vienna will be between March and May. This is the time of the year when everything is in full bloom, and the temperature is mild and pleasant. Unlike summer, there are only a few tourists who come to Vienna during the season so you can enjoy sightseeing sans the crowd. You'll also find much lower prices for accommodation at this time of year.

Vienna has four seasons with each season playing an important role in the Viennese lifestyle.

Summer – June/July/August Summer is Vienna at

its brightest and when the temperature is at its highest. There are 8 hours of sunlight each day which can give you the chance to explore and enjoy the city. If travelling in summer, it's always a great idea to carry some water with you as the heat may be intense at times, although do note that the summer here is not nearly as intense as you'd find further down in the Mediterranean region. In fact, even in the peak of the summer season, in August, temps will barely reach 25°C (77°F).

Autumn – September/October/November
Autumn or Fall happens during the months of September to November. The skies can be overcast for most days yet the changing of colors, in the surrounding forests, make this a fantastic time to visit if you wish to take a few day trips out of town and explore the countryside.

Winter – December/January/February The winter months are from December to February, with January being the coldest. The temperature can drop down to a low of -3 degrees Celsius (26 degrees Fahrenheit) with only 2 hours of bright sunshine in an average day, it can be a dreary time to visit. This season is characterized by snowfall, strong winds and sometimes patches of rain. Be ready for heavy frosts and snow drifts around the city. December is a brilliant time to experience the amazing Christmas Markets of Vienna, renowned throughout Europe as some of the very best. Palaces and parks are set up to become Christmas villages. Choirs sing their Christmas carols and the scent of Christmas epicurean fare is everywhere. Aside from this burst of color, however, Vienna's most popular sites (like palaces and gardens) are in shut-down mode. Most statues are covered for winter and gardens lay bare, so if you do wish to spend much time outdoors this may not be the right season for you.

Spring – March/April/May This is the most comfortable season in Vienna. The city will be bursting with colors as the temperature remains cool and mild without the snow. There is an average of 9 degrees Celsius (48 degrees Fahrenheit) at the start of this season. April is the month when locals celebrate St. George's Day, the patron Saint of England who is also the patron saint of horses. You can catch performances at the Spanish Riding School, and there are a number of concerts in some other venues in the city. March marks the onset of Spring and this season lasts until May. Easter is a wonderful celebration to experience here at this time. This is also the time when you can try the "Osterbock", their traditional beer specialty. A lot of special performances which are mostly in celebration of Easter, are held in several concert venues in the city.

Language

The official language in Austria is German, with High German spoken by the great majority of people and *Weinerisch*, a local dialect, spoken by most Viennese. Austrian-German sounds much "softer" then the one spoken in Germany, although many foreigners will not be able to tell the difference.

Austrians put a high premium on education. In schools, English is taught extensively and it is considered the accepted second language, thus communicating with locals, especially in the capital, will not be an issue.

Getting In

Major international airlines and carriers fly directly to **Vienna International Airport** daily. This modern and compact terminal is only 11 miles southeast of Vienna and is accessible via direct transport links.

http://www.viennaairport.com/en/passengers

Major airlines from the US have direct flights to Vienna. Austrian Airlines and Turkish Airlines fly direct from New York and Washington. Austrian Airlines and American Airlines fly direct from Chicago and Virgin Atlantic and British Airways fly direct from Las Vegas. Air Canada flies direct from Orlando, Fort Myers, Denver, Detroit, Philadelphia, San Francisco and Charlotte.

Reaching the city from the airport

Taxis are readily available and cost around €35-40 for two to three passengers. You can also pre-book transfers for a cheaper rate of about €29. Buses connect to the airport with two main railway terminals. The **Vienna S-bahn** (commuter train) **line S7** links the airport and city with many stops in different districts. Regular fare is only €4.20, including a connection to the U-bahn network. The

City Airport Train (CAT) links the airport with Wien Mitte station in around 16 minutes (non-stop) and costs €12 one way or €19 return.

Getting Around

The city's immediate historic centre is best explored on foot. However, Vienna has one of the most organized, highly-developed public transport systems in the world, ideal for anyone who wants to explore a little further.

BY PUBLIC TRANSPORT

- Buses, trams and trains are punctual, reliable and far-reaching, and flat-fare tickets are interchangeable between them all. Their combined comprehensive itineraries mean that you have public transport available to you, in one form or another, 24 hours a day.

- Single-fares cost €2.20 and include as many transfers as needed. A 24-hour ticket costs €7.60 and 48 hours, €13.30.

- If you're planning on taking more than two trips a day on the public transport, then it may be wise to purchase a Vienna Card, which gives you unlimited transport as well as discounts to attractions, museums, shops and restaurants. A 48-hour card costs €18.90 and 72 –hour card only €21.90. Do note that this card is only worthwhile should you wish to utilize the great majority of discounts offered. Do note that one adult card includes one child under the age of 15 years.

http://www.wien.info/en/travel-info/vienna-card

- Remember to always validate your ticket at your first point of embarkation - whether it be bus, train or tram. Failure to do so can incur a €100 fine.

- The underground train system, U-Bahn, is the most popular to get around the city. It boasts five lines and reaches the great majority of important sites. The regional S-Bahn can also be useful when travelling out of town.

- Trams are a slower, but much more scenic, way to get around town.

- The entire rail system shuts down between just after midnight and about 4 am. A comprehensive fleet of night-buses (called "NightLiners") pick up the slack. Note that standard tickets are accepted on the night buses.

- On a side note, keep in mind that doors of buses/trams/trains do not automatically open at a designated stop. You must press the 'open door' button or, better still, step behind a local the first few times, to learn about timing.

BY TAXI

Taxis here are (relatively) inexpensive, so if you're travelling in a group it may be worth your while to jump in a cab instead of a train, as long as you're travelling outside of peak-times. Do ask for the estimated fare, and also request for the meter to be turned on. Should you wish to hire a taxi for a whole day (for an out of city excursion, for example), feel free to barter for a set daily rate. This is perfectly acceptable.

BY BYCICLE

You may also explore the city and the countryside by bike, something most locals do on a regular basis. This is a very convenient and fast way to enjoy the sights of Vienna! There are 1,200 kms of cycle paths in the city and you can rent bikes from several stations in the city. You can find more info and cool tips below.

Bike Info: http://tinyurl.com/bikeinfovienna

Vienna Cycling Guide: http://tinyurl.com/viennacycling

2 OVERVIEW OF VIENNA'S NEIGHBORHOODS

Vienna is a large, sprawling city yet the most interesting sites for tourists are relatively close to one another. But that's not to say that staying outside the immediate centre, would not be worth your while. Suburban Vienna is very beautiful and each of the 23 districts which make up this metropolis has unique character. Districts are known both by name and number, with the first 9 being the city's inner suburbs and, most likely, the ones you'll explore at length.

Innere Stadt (District 1) – Home to the **Old Town**, and where the Habsburgs built their residence. This is the best place to stay in if visiting for only a few days, as it is centrally located and pedestrian friendly. This district is home to the **Hofburg Palace, St Stephen's Cathedral, the Spanish Riding School**, among other popular sights you should see.

Leopoldstadt (District 2) – This district is

technically an island in the middle of the Danube, and home to the famous Vienna Ferris wheel (**Wiener Riesenrad**). The district is easily accessible from Innere Stadt by U-Bahn, and is also where you can find the **Prater Park**, a public amusement park. This area used to be home to the largest population of Jews in the city, prior to WWII.

Landstrasse (District 3) – Home to the **Belvedere Palace**, the 3rd District has its share of history as the place where Richard the Lionheart was captured during the Third Crusade. This area is mostly residential and aside from Belvedere, you can also find the **Schwarzenberg Palace** and **Wien Mitte** rail station.

Weiden (District 4) – A trendy neighborhood with historic buildings in a small neighborhood center. **St. Charles Church** can be found here as well as the **Viennese History Museum**.

Margareten (District 5) – This is a residential district but is also frequented by tourists to see the **historic homes** of Vienna's more famous people. **Margaretenplatz** also offers a diverse dining experience from the basic Austrian cuisine to other international delicacies.

Mariahilf (District 6) – If you like shopping this district is for you. This area is the home to one of the busiest shopping streets in Vienna, the **Mariahilferstrasse**, and also home to a produce market (**Naschmarkt**) and flea market

(**Flohmarkt**).

Neubau (District 7) – The place of quirky shops and homey cafés. This area has **artist studios, clothing and housewares shops**, traditional Viennese and carry-out restaurants, music clubs and bars. Most **museums** in Vienna are located here.

Josefstadt (District 8) – The eighth district is the place for those looking for a place "somewhere quiet" where you can find a number of cafés and restaurants. **Schönborn Palace** is located here. There are also many backyard stages and small theaters in this district.

Alsergund (District 9) – Dubbed as the young and modern district of Vienna due to the influx of students from all over the world, this is the **university hood** of Vienna.

Organized City Tours

If you need help trying to get around the city, why not join an organized tour to get your bearings while learning the history of the city? From walking tours to Segway and cycling, Vienna plays host to an infinite array of super fun, affordable and very educational tours. From history to food tours, architecture, palaces and even hiking tours to nearby forests, there's a tour here to suit all tastes and budgets.

Here are some of our favorites:

Big Bus Tour Vienna – The Austrian version of

this international favorite is a big hit with first-time visitors, and for very good reason. The bus itineraries are comprehensive and the guides very knowledgeable and helpful. The various lines cover the city's main sites and can get you out into the wine growing region of Vienna's outer suburbs. A 24-hour ticket includes two free walking tours and a Danube River cruise, which is just phenomenal value.

http://eng.bigbustours.com/vienna/home.html

Pedalpower Bike & Segway – This super popular tour agency organizes bicycle and Segway tours, as well as bike rental for those who are confident enough to go it alone. Their Wachau Valley Tour, a full-day affair out into Vienna's countryside, past vineyards and historic villages, is one of the best sellers and highly recommended to anyone with a little more energy and time.

https://www.pedalpower.at/

Wienguide Tours – If you don't mind splurging a little, or are travelling with a group of friends or family, then these guys are for you. Wienguide offer arguably the best private tours in Vienna and will take you anywhere you want to go, for any length of time, in whatever language you need.

http://www.wienguide.net/vienna-guide-english/

PolaWalk – The quirky concept of Polaroid photographic tours have really taken off in Vienna, and are now rated among the best in the city. You get an Instant Polaroid camera, a dozen shots to take, a comprehensive lesson on exposure/lighting/angles and a wonderfully comprehensive city tour to boot. Plus, you get to keep all your pics!

http://www.polawalk.com/en/

Discover Vienna Tours – A large, professional and well-established tour agency which runs tours in several European cities. Choose from city or winery tours, multi-day adventures and evening walking tours.

http://discoverviennatours.com

Self-guided walking tours – If you're travelling on a tight budget, or simply wish to tour the city at your own pace, download one of the excellent self-guided walking tour maps you can find on:

BigBoyTravel

http://tinyurl.com/bigboytravelvienna

Mozart Walk (click on the Mozart Walk Download link)

http://tinyurl.com/mozartwalkvienna

National Geographic Art Tour

http://tinyurl.com/natgeovienna

(Insider's Tip: If you want to enjoy a tour for only 2 Euros, then hop on tram #1. You'll get a wonderful

tour of the inner city and get to ride on a historic tram at the same time!)

3 HOW TO GET YOUR BEARINGS AND AVOID GETTING LOST

Vienna may be a sprawling city, but what makes it unique is that it boasts a modern city center void of skyscrapers or giant towering office buildings. Nestled between the Wienerwald (Viennese Woods), and the Donau (Danube River), this is a very picturesque city where water and forest views can be enjoyed from almost every corner.

Most tourist spots are centered in the Old Town of Vienna. We'll give you some brief orientation guides of this compact centre before moving on to the bigger confines of the city itself. Download and print a city map (http://tinyurl.com/getmapvienna) and have it at hand when you read the following tips.

- The Old Town is bordered by the following streets:

Northwest -   Schottenring

West: Dr K Rennerring & Dr K Luegerring

Northeast: Franz Josefs Kai

East: Schubertiring, Parkring and Stubenring

South: Openring, Burgring, and Karnnering

- This area is collectively known as **The Ring**, and right in the center of the ring is **St Stephen's Cathedral**. No matter where you go, as long as you know the streets that comprise the ring & see the cathedral within your line of sight, you'll know you're still within the Old Town. It is extremely difficult to get utterly lost in the Old Town.

- It also helps that in the north side of the Ring, you have the Danube snaking through the city center. If you see the river directly in front of you, chances are that you are in the South (where the Old Town is). If however, you find yourself walking away from the Danube then that means you are heading north and away from the Old Town.

- If you plan to go outside of the Old Town, your guiding point will be the U-Bahn. There are multiple stops covered by various lines, and within the stations, you can see big maps telling you where you are in the city, what line is available at that stop or what train is passing through. U-Bahns are a great way to get your bearings if you are feeling lost or need to get back to a specific location near your hotel, simply head to the nearest train station, where you can find a comprehensive city map.

- When in doubt, whip out your city map, approach a local with a warm smile and ask him/her to point to where you are. You'll find locals here more than obliging in this regard.

- Always carry the business card of your hotel, should you get *really* desperately lost. You can either hop on a taxi to a popular spot you are familiar with, or take one back to your hotel.

- Each U-Bahn station has several street exits so do your homework before heading out, and know exactly on which street you're supposed to exit. This could make all the difference!

- Most Museums are free of charge on the first Sunday of every month (excluding temporary exhibitions)

- Before leaving home, head to the iTunes store and download this amazing app (AnachB), which works like a public-transport-google-map for Vienna. Simply input your current location (you may need a local's help if you are lost), enter the spot you wish to reach and within seconds you'll have all public transport options (and directions) at your fingertips. http://tinyurl.com/anachbvienna

Tourist Information offices

Tourist Information (TI) kiosks are a godsend both for info before heading out into the city and utilize the free WiFi to download maps. It should be noted that Vienna boasts arguably some of the nicest-looking TI offices we've ever seen!

You'll find more info on the official website

(http://www.wien.info/en) and, if you wish to call them ahead of time, simply dial +43 1 24555. Here are the three main branches:

Vienna Airport Arrival Hall - Open from 7 am -10 pm

Main Train Station (Haupftbahnhof) - Open from 9am – 5pm

Albertinaplatz/Maysedergasse - Open 9am – 7 pm

Useful Maps & Websites

The maps and links provided so far will hopefully go a long way in ensuring your vacation runs as smoothly as possible.

But wait…there's more!

Here are some more resourceful links and downloadable maps you may find useful:

ViennaInfo : official Vienna tourism website
https://www.wien.info/en

Sightseeing Map: a detailed map of the city with the most prominent landmarks marked

http://www.city-walks.info/Vienna/Map.html

EbookMap: application for downloading city map to e-book readers

http://www.ebookmaps.com/en/vienna-maps-for-ebook-readers-en.php

Offmaps: great map app for iPhones, iPads and iPods

http://offmaps.com/

ViennaPass: 48 and 72 hour cards which includes unlimited public transport rides and a whole host of discounts on attractions, sites, restaurants and shops

http://www.viennapass.com

MetroMap: a detailed map of the city's metro system, including U and S-Bahn trains, and trams

http://tinyurl.com/metromapvienna

AirportTrain: info on the CAT which plies the route between the city's centre and the international airport

http://tinyurl.com/viennacat

AirBnB: rent a room or entire holiday apartment or villa in Vienna

https://www.airbnb.com/s/Vienna--Austria

4 TOP 20 ATTRACTIONS IN VIENNA

Vienna's historic centre, known as District 1, is an absolute delight to explore at length and this is no doubt where you'll be spending most of your time. Strolling, cycling and even jogging along the Danube Canal is a favorite pastime of the Viennese, and something you definitely should not miss experiencing. Although not as picturesque as Paris' riverfront, Vienna's riverside is a relaxing and quite green place to discover on foot. Canal cruises abound and are quite affordable, so although the canal is definitely not the prettiest part of Vienna (by far!) it's worthwhile hopping on a riverboat and cruising for an hour or so.

Following are Vienna's top 20 tourist attractions:

Hofburg Palace –This stunning palace in the center of Vienna was home to Sisi. Here, you'll find the Sisi Museum, Imperial Apartments & the Treasury. Part of the palace is still used by the current Austrian President.

Address: Michaelerkuppel, DISTRICT 1

Hours: 9 am – 6 pm (5.30 pm in autumn & winter)

(Insider's Tip: head to the Hofburg Chapel at 9 am on a Sunday and you can enjoy a performance by the world-renowned Vienna Boys Choir, free of charge!)

http://www.hofburg-wien.at/en.html

Schönbrunn Palace – A UNESCO World Heritage site, this was the former summer palace of the Habsburgs, and is now one of the country's most important landmarks. The Baroque architecture is simply splendid.

Address: Michaelerkuppel, DISTRICT 1

Hours: 8:30 am – 5:30 pm

(Insider's Tip: Schönbrunn Palace often hosts amazing concerts on weekends and, aside the famed Opera House, this is the most magnificent settings in the whole country to enjoy a superb opera concert)

http://www.schoenbrunn.at/

The Belvedere – The home of former Austrian Empress Maria Theresa is an expansive palace and garden complex, with a beautiful Orangerie and Royal Stables.

Address: Prinze Eugen-Strasse 27, DISTRICT 3

Hours: 10 am – 6 pm

http://www.belvedere.at/en

St Stephen's Cathedral – Built from the ruins of two churches, this nearly 900-year old cathedral is one of the great religious symbols of Vienna. Its highlights are the towers and the brilliantly colored roof, adorned with thousands of mosaic tiles.

Address: Stephansplatz 3, DISTRICT 1

Hours: 6 am – 10 pm

https://www.stephanskirche.at

Museums Quarter – One of the largest cultural areas in the world, the Museum Quarter contains a wide variety of museums, boasting both new and historic architecture.

Address: Museumsplatz 1, DISTRICT 7

(Insider's Tip: This is probably Vienna's trendiest 'hang out' spots, where make-shift open-air bars and huge couches are set up in outdoor plazas. Head here on a weekend and chill out with the city's art students for a bit of hippie fun)

http://www.mqw.at/en/

Kunsthistorisches Museum (Museum of Art History) – Vienna's foremost museum, housed in a striking 19th century palace, built to house the private collections of the Habsburgs.

Address: Maria-Theresien Platz DISTRICT 1

Hours: 10 am to 6 pm

http://www.khm.at/en/

Tiergarten Schönbrunn (Schönbrunn Zoo) – The oldest zoo in the world, established in 1752, started as a private Royal menagerie and is found next door to the Schönbrunn Palace. Many times voted Europe's very best zoo, it is a must for animal lovers.

Address: Maxingstraße 13b, DISTRICT 13

Hours: 9 am -6.30 pm

https://www.zoovienna.at/en/zoo-and-visitors/visitor-information/

Rathaus – The imposing, Neo-Gothic Rathaus building is home Vienna's City Council and other administrative functions.

Address: Friedrich-Schmidt-Platz 1, DISTRICT 1

Hours: 8 am – 6 pm (closed on weekends)

http://www.wien.gv.at/verwaltung/rathaus/index.html

Wiener Riesenrad – A 200-foot Ferris wheel in the Prater Amusement Park, this is one of the iconic symbols of the city.

Address: Riesenradplatz 1, DISTRICT 2

http://www.wienerriesenrad.com/en

Vienna State Opera – This is a historic opera building, dating back to the 19th century and is regarded as one of the world's best. Both the interior and exterior façades are simply spellbinding. If you can, try to catch a concert here during your stay, it will make for an unforgettable experience.

Address: Opernring 2, DISTRICT 1

(Insider's Tip: If you're on a tight budget, simply show up at the Opera House two hours before the start of any show, and you can score standing room tickets for less than 10 Euros!)

http://www.wiener-staatsoper.at

Naturhistorisches Museum (Natural History Museum) – Take a virtual tour of this museum on their website and you'll discover why this is rated as one of the world's best natural history museums. There are over 94,000 square feet of exhibitions here, with collections which began almost three centuries ago. An absolute must if travelling with kids.

Address: Burgring 7, DISTRICT 1

Hours: 9 am – 6.30 pm

Spanish Riding School – A traditional riding school for the beautiful Lipizzan horses. The performances at the school are open to the public and boast some of the most difficult maneuvers in the riding world. This school has been operating for more than 450 years.

Address: Michaelerplatz 1, DISTRICT 1

Hours: Performances are usually held twice a week

(Insider's Tip: Head here on a Sunday at about 10.45 am and you'll see the magnificent Stallions parading down the street as they make their way between riding halls. It's a fantastic photo op and it's free!)

http://www.srs.at/en_US/start-en/

Albertina Museum – If you're a fan of old-school print drawings and old master prints, then this museum is for you. It contains over 1 million exhibits, including works by Picasso, Monet and Matisse.

Address: Albertinaplatz 1, DISTRICT 1

Hours: 10 am-6 pm

(Insider's Tip: Just outside the Albertina Museum you'll find one of the city's most famous sausage stands! Great for a quick snack either before or after your museum visit)

http://www.albertina.at/en

Karlskirche (St. Charles' Church) – A Baroque church with a beautiful dome and bas-relief elements; it is also find the final resting place of the famous composer Antonio Vivaldi.

Address: Kreuzherrengasse 1, DISTRICT 4

Hours: 9 am – 6 pm

http://www.karlskirche.at/

Hundertwasserhaus – A very colorful and contemporary apartment building in the Landstrase District, that's worth a closer look.

Address: Kegelgasse 36-38, DISTRICT 3

http://www.hundertwasser-haus.info/en/

Imperial Crypt - A 400 year old burial chamber that contains the bodies of Empress Maria Theresa's family.

Address: Tegetthoffstraße 2, DISTRICT 1

Hours: 10:00 am – 6:00 pm

http://www.kaisergruft.at/

Donauturm (Danube Tower) – A great observation tower with sweeping views of Vienna.

Address: Donauturmstraße 4, DISTRICT 22

Hours: 10:00 am – Midnight

http://www.donauturm.at/en/

Volksgarten (People's Garden) – A vast very beautiful public park which is part of the Hofburg Palace.

Address: Volksgarten, DISTRICT 1

Hours: 9 am – 6 pm

http://www.hofburg-wien.at/en.html

Burgtheater – The 2nd oldest theater in Europe, the Burgtheater runs over 800 performances every year, and has an elaborate façade carved into the main entrance.

Address: Universitätsring 2, DISTRICT 1

http://www.burgtheater.at/Content.Node2/home/eninfo/English_Information.at.php

Maria-Theresien Platz – A beautiful public square notable for the statue of Empress Maria Theresa.

Address: DISTRICT 1

Aside admiring the city's main historical and cultural attractions, hiking around eth outskirts of the city is one of the most enjoyable things you can do. There are over 500 kms of hiking trails built within the forests, and most are in the heart of the city's most protected recreational areas. Being Europe's 'greenest' city means that getting out into nature here is infinitely easy.

5 DAILY ITINERARY PLANNER & DAY ONE

Vienna on a long weekend

Vienna is one of those cities you could visit every year, for two decades, and never find yourself lost for things to see and do. That's wonderful if you live nearby but a bit daunting if a vacation to Vienna happens to be a once-in-a-lifetime treat. What to do first? Can Vienna be done in just a weekend? Well of course it can, as long as you prioritize, put on your (nice looking) walking shoes and make the most of every minute in this superb city.

Following is our sample itinerary, to give you an idea of just how much (or how little) you can expect to fill into your Vienna vacation days.

Day 1 in Vienna

Start your day in the city centre and take in the most famous sites first.

St. Stephen's Cathedral

Let's start at the Cathedral, located right in the heart of the city. Are you ready to climb 343 steps? Once you reach the top of the 450-feet tower, you'll be greeted by a magnificent view of the city. This is quite a prize for the sweat of climbing up those challenging stairs! You will be amazed not just with the view but also with the beauty of this impressive architectural piece. This church is one of the most important edifices in Vienna, built over 800 years ago. Its interiors contain gothic and baroque-inspired décor, created by several European artists reflecting the Renaissance era of the 1500's. The centerpiece is a painting on the main altar dedicated to St. Stephen depicting Catholic martyrdom. This centerpiece on the high altar represents the stoning of the church's patron, St. Stephen. It is framed by figures of patron saints from the surrounding areas and surmounted with a statue of St. Mary. The church suffered heavily during World War II but was restored with the outpouring of financial support from the public. Today, this massive architectural piece stands as a symbol of Austria's freedom and free spirit.

What: St Stephen's Cathedral

Where: Stephan's Platz 3 – DISTRICT 1

Directions: One block east of the Stephansplatz U-Bahn stop, between Singer and Schulkestrasses

When: Mon – Sat: 6:00am – 10:00pm/ Sun and holidays: 7:00am-10pm

How Much: Church is free to visit. Guided tour €4.50 – catacombs, €4.50 - south tower, €3.50 - elevator to Pummerin bell, €4.50. Combined ticket, €14.50

Suggested arrival time & duration: 9 am – 1 hour (do note that guided tours are timed so check website before visiting)

Hofburg Palace

Want to get a glimpse of what Vienna Royalty life was like in the 15th century? Hofburg Palace will give you just that! The palace was once the center of Habsburg dynasty, the most powerful family which ruled the Austria-Hungary Empire from 1200's to the early 1900's. This dynasty produced most of the kings who ruled Western Europe for several decades. You will be impressed with the luxury and trappings of the old world monarchy's residence which holds timeless regal furnishing and decor. One thing that you should not miss seeing is the Imperial Silver Collection. This is a museum dedicated to the symbols of royal opulence, the facilities and tableware that were once used by the royal members of this dynasty. Parts of the palace are nowadays this also the residence of the Austrian President.

What: Hofburg Palace

Where: Michaelerkyppel, DISTRICT 1

Directions: Only three blocks east of St Stephen's Cathedral, the closest U-Bahn stations are

Stephansplatz and Herrengasse

When: 9 am – 5.30 pm

How Much: Adults €12.50 - children (aged 6-18) €7.50 - students (aged 19-25) €11.50 add €3 for audio guide.

Suggested arrival time & duration: 10 am – 2 hours

Spanish Riding School

Very near the Hofburg Palace is the world-famous Spanish Riding School (Spanische Hofreitschule). This is the place where Lipizzaner stallions hold equestrian performances accompanied by classical music. Watching this one-of-a-kind performance, you will be taken back to the years of the imperial Habsburg era. The horses dance in complete synchronicity with the baroque music being played giving you a world-class performance. Don't miss the hanging glistening chandeliers and the elegant interiors. As one of Vienna's top attractions, you may need to book tickets in advance to have guaranteed seats.

What: Spanish Riding School

Where: Michaelerplatz, DISTRICT 1

Directions: Just one block south of the Herrengasse U-Bahn station

When: Shows usually held twice a week- check schedule before visiting

How Much: €23 - €130; morning training €12

Suggested arrival time & duration: 12 pm – 1 hour

Time for Lunch

It's lunchtime! Time to take a pick from one of the nearby restaurants in the area where you can savor some of Vienna's culinary delights. One of the best choices is **Esterhazykeller Restaurant**. This charming restaurant has an outdoor café and an underground cellar type dining area. They offer traditional Viennese foods which include "Weinerschnitzel", a very thin, breaded and deep fried veal schnitzel (boneless meat coated with flour and beaten eggs with bread crumbs), an array of salads, wine and "Apfelstrudel", a Viennese version of the apple pie. Prices here are quite reasonable and you can enjoy your food amidst a very classy and traditional Viennese ambiance.

What: Esterhazykeller Restaurant

Where: Haarhof 1, DISTRICT 1

Directions: One block east of herrengasse U-Bahn station, down a small alleyway

When: Outdoor area open 11 am to midnight, downstairs cellar from 4 pm onwards

How Much: Less than €10 for a lunch-time special

Suggested arrival time & duration: 1 pm – 1 hour

Imperial Treasury

Are you ready to discover what the royals wore during their golden time? Step inside one of the famous museums in Vienna…and find out. Located inside the courtyard of Hofburg Palace is the Imperial Treasury, considered one of the world's most comprehensive. Over six century of Crown Jewels are exhibited, making this arguably the most impressive section of the entire palace. The treasury boasts 21 rooms showcasing crowns, gowns, robes, cloaks, scepters and thrones of the imperial Habsburg dynasty. This is the largest and the perhaps the most impressive treasury in the world. It contains auspicious and grand pieces including an imperial crown studded with hundreds of precious jewels and gemstones, and the largest cut emerald in the world. These are all priceless treasures representing only a portion of the Habsburg Dynasty's wealth! The most important piece in this treasury is the holy lance or nail which they say was the one which pierced and nailed the right hand of Jesus Christ to the cross. How it made it into the hands of the Habsburgs is still a mystery.

What: Imperial Treasury

Where: Hofburg Palace Courtyard

Directions: See above

When: 9 am – 5.30 pm

How Much: €12 – audio guide €4

Suggested arrival time & duration: 1 pm – 1 hour

Art History Museum (Kunsthistorisches)

Just across the Hofburg Palace is the Art History Museum which looks like a chocolate box wrapped in gold. You will be greeted by the statue of Empress Maria Theresa, the longest running monarch who ruled the empire for over 40 years. Once inside, you will see the painting on the ceiling depicting the great artists of all times – Michaelangelo, Leonardo and many more. Art lovers with be enthralled by the vast collection of great masterpieces created by world-famous painters and sculptors from Europe, as well Egypt and Greece. There are a number of works from the Netherlands, Italy, France and Germany (acquired during the 17th century when the Habsburg dynasty was spreading its empire). Various works by Reubens, Rembrandt, Raphael, Albrecht Durer, and Pieter Bruegel are found here.

What: Art History Museum

Where: Maria Theresien Platz, DISTRICT 1

Directions: Only one block north of the Museumquartier U-Bahn stop

When: Tues, Wed, and Fri –Sun 10:00 am – 6:00 pm; Thu 10:00 am – 9:00 pm

How Much: €14

Suggested arrival time & duration: 2.10 pm – 2 hours

Naschmarkt

After exploring a few historical treasure sites, it's time for you to take a break – at Vienna's most famous, largest and busiest marketplace, the Naschmarkt. This bustling market has over 150 stalls selling wide array of goods from fruits, vegetables, flowers, pastries, bread, cheese, spices, herbs, balsamic products and a whole lot more. Naschmarkt used to be a farmer's market back in the 18th century.

This market sells culinary goods and hard-to-find products from all over the world and, on Saturdays, also includes a fantastic flea-market. Here, you'll get to sample and taste the different varieties of food and get tips on how you can make them yourself right in your own home. Nibble on some Viennese pastries and other goodies. Even if you're not a foodie, you will enjoy this tour as it will give you a first-hand experience and a tangible taste of Viennese street commerce.

What: Naschmarkt

Where: Wienzeile, DISTRICT 6

Directions: Right between Karlsplatz and Kettenbruckengasse, which has a U-Bahn station

When: 9 am – 6.30 pm

Suggested arrival time & duration: 4.30 pm – 2 hours

Schönbrunn Palace (Optional destination for

daily itinerary)

An alternative stop during your day is Schönbrunn, the majestic palace of Vienna which was built in the late 18th century. This medieval palace is undoubtedly one of the architectural prides of Vienna. As it is considered to be the tourist attraction of the city, you don't want to miss seeing this place. This is the summer palace of the Habsburg monarchy. Inside are a number of attractions hidden within its grounds which include a zoo, lakes, fountains, fake ruins, statues, and greenhouses. The extensive, well-kept gardens extend to over a square kilometer of grassy lawns lined with trees, woods and adorned with colorful flowerbeds in various hues.

Schönbrunn Palace has been open to the public since 1779. This is a UNESCO World Heritage Site with over a thousand rooms, but only a few are open for public viewing. The palace is about 20kms out of the inner city and will take about 20 minutes to reach it by train.

What: Schönbrunn Palace

Where: Schönbrunner Schloßstraße 47, DISTRICT 13

Directions: Reach the palace by U-Bahn, alighting at 'Schönbrunn'

When: 8.30 am – 5.30 pm

How Much: €12.90, €15.90 for an audio-guided

tour, €18.90 for a real guided tour

Suggested arrival time & duration: We suggest you arrive here in the early afternoon, to avoid the large morning tour-group crowds.

So that's it for your first day in Vienna. It was quite an amazing experience with tons of exciting discoveries. If you've managed to complete all of the above-recommended activities…well done!

6 DAY 2 IN VIENNA

Fresh from a busy head start of your inner city tour yesterday, on your second day in Vienna, you'll get to explore other parts of the city. Again, the places that you will visit are planned to maximize your time so walking from one to the other is quite easy.

Why not start the day with a nice, sumptuous breakfast at **Corto & Nero**? They have the best bread and pastries in Vienna! Must-try include poppy seed chocolate tarts and homemade brownies which go down well with a blended coffee. The atmosphere here is cozy, without much fuss, yet chic and urban. All the food here is made from local ingredients and is always freshly made.

What: Corto e Nero

Where: Wiedner Hauptstrasse 48, DISTRICT 4

Directions: Take the U-Bahn (line 10) to Taubstummengasse, take the north exit, turn left at Floragasse and left again at Weidner Hauptstrasse. The café is on the left hand side.

When: 7 am – 9 pm

How Much: Between €10 and €20 for a full breakfast

Suggested arrival time & duration: 9 am – 1 hour

http://tinyurl.com/cnvienna

Belvedere Palace

Built in early 1700's, Belvedere palace was built for a military strategist, Prince Eugene of Savoy, conqueror of the Turks. Belvedere was the Prince's summer residence. It has two sections – the Upper (Oberes) which has an Orangery, and lower part (Unteres) which served as the venue for banquets and other big events. Both are connected by a long, landscaped garden. This palace houses great Austrian artistic works from the Middle Ages up to the modern days. It also boasts world-class art collections and many French impressionist works since the Prince was originally from France, and an avid collector. Belvedere boasts fine rococo interiors and decorations. Belvedere means "beautiful view" and this palace offers exactly that. You may even take a small walk on the Belvedere slope to catch a glimpse of the city and to enjoy the gardens and the pond.

What: Belvedere Palace

Where: Prinz EugenStrasse 27, DISTRICT 3

Directions: From Corto e Nero you can reach the palace by walking back towards the U-Bahn station and continuing east for two blocks. The southern end of the estate is also only two block east of the Wien Hauptbahnhof U-Bahn terminal.

When: 10:00 am to 6:00 pm

How Much: €26 (includes upper, lower, Orangerie & Winter Palace)

Suggested arrival time & duration: 10 am – 2.5 hours

Stadtpark

From an elegant palace, you will continue your leisurely walk to a park in the heart of Vienna, the Stadtpark. Established in 1862, this park has been laid out in an open, sloping terrain in an English landscape style. Stadtpark abounds with blooms and foliage, bursting with colors set amidst the greens. Several fountains also dot the park making it a perfect place to sit down and relax. The Wein River, a small branch of the Donau River with fast flowing waters, cuts through the park. Inside this park is the Kursalon Pavilion which was originally a spa, but was converted into a concert venue. Today, this is where musical concerts playing the music of Strauss and Mozart are regularly held.

This park also has a large number of monuments, sculptures and statues of famous musical geniuses and masters like Schubert, Lehar, Stoltz and Beethoven. At the center of the park is the gilded, bronze statue of Johann Strauss Junior, the Waltz King.

What: Stadtpark

Where: Parkring, DISTRICT 3

Directions: The park is on the eastern fringes of the inner ring road, to the west of Wien Mitte U-Bahn station.

When: Anytime

Suggested arrival time & duration: 1 pm – 1 hour

Albertina Art Museum

This museum used to be the Habsburg apartment for guests who would visit from abroad. Now, it houses the greatest graphic art collection in the world. It safeguards over 50,000 drawings and watercolors, and 900,000 graphic art works from the late Gothic era to the present.

Famous pieces and works of Leonardo da Vinci, Michelangelo Buonarroti, and Raphael Santi are all found here. There are also the masterpieces of French impressionists Manet and Renoir, as well as Austria's own Egon Schiele and Gustav Klimt. The large graphic art collection is arranged in chronological order with some prized pieces dating back to the early 1500s. Aside from paintings, this museum also holds a large number of architectural and photographic collections.

What: Albertina Art Museum

Where: Albertinaplatz 1, DISTRICT 1

Directions: Following the ring road to the west, you will come across Operngasse Street (on the right) which will lead you straight up to the museum square. The closest U-Bahn station is that at Karlsplatz.

When: 10 am– 6 pm

How Much: €12.90

Suggested arrival time & duration: 2 pm - 2.5 hours

Schmetterlinghaus - The Butterfly House

About 200 meters away from the Vienna Opera House is a tropical haven created for the gentlest flying creatures on earth. You'll be mesmerized by over 400 species of colorful butterflies flying freely over falls, flowers and plants in an environment created as close as possible to their natural habitat. This stunning Art Noveau palm houses was built at the beginning of the last century. This is actually a part of the Hofburg Palace, situated at the edge of the Burggarten palace gardens. A place so peaceful and quiet, it provides a perfect respite as you enjoy the tranquil surroundings of this location. Some butterflies may even land on your head as if greeting you and welcoming your visit to this sanctuary.

What: Schmetterlinghaus

Where: Am Schmetterlinghaus, DISTRICT 1

Directions: Only 100 north of the Albertina Museum

When: 10 am – 4.45 pm (weekdays), 3.45 pm weekends

How Much: Adults €6, Seniors €5, Students €4.5, Children (3 - 16) €3

Suggested arrival time & duration: 4.30 pm – 1 hour

Staatsoper – Vienna's State Opera House

The world's most beautiful and respected opera house has been drawing its curtains for well over one hundred and thirty years and is the piece de resistance along Vienna's centre ring road. The building is neo-Renaissance in style with a number of allegorical figures symbolizing the liberal arts. The internationally acclaimed Vienna Philharmonic Orchestra recruits its members from this opera house.

What: Staatsoper

Where: Openring 2, DISTRICT 1

Directions: Two blocks north of Karlsplatz U-Bahn station, along Karntner Strasse.

When: Guided tours are held several times a day

How Much: €7.50 for a guided tour **Highly recommended

Suggested arrival time & duration: Arrive here at 5.30 pm and, if there is a concert, you can score cheap standing room tickets!

Musikverein (alternative option)

Cap your second day in Vienna with a visit to Musikverein, a concert hall which is home to the world famous Vienna Philharmonic Orchestra. Considered one of the three finest concert halls in the world, it boasts of highly regarded acoustics. This hall was inaugurated by Emperor Franz Joseph in 1870. It also serves as the venue of the annual Vienna's New Year Concert. This air-conditioned hall has 1,744 seats and standing room for 300 people.

What: Musikverein

Where: Musikvereinplatz, DISTRICT 1

Directions: Just 100 metres south of Karlsplatz U-Bahn Station

When: Time of tours vary depending on concert itinerary – check website before visiting: http://tinyurl.com/musikvereintour

How Much: Guided visits cost €6 pp. and last 45 minutes

Suggested arrival time & duration: 5.30 pm – 1 hour

7 DAY 3 IN VIENNA

Danube's Wachau Valley

On your last day in Vienna, you can enjoy a full day excursion to the spectacular, and UNESCO Heritage Listed, **Wachau Valley of the Danube**. You can take a boat trip down the Danube from Melk to Krems, admiring charming villages lined up along the river banks, and the steep vineyards and old castles which make this region so very unique. The Danube River flows 2,000 miles across 10 countries, starting at the Black Forest in Germany and winding its way to the Black Sea. This is Europe's longest river, and the most romantic and scenic part of it is here, in Austria.

At the old wine town of Krems, Wachau is picture-perfect. You'll see medieval castles perched atop hills above the river, in scenes reminiscent of historic legends and myths. The most famous Wachau Valley village is Durnstein. This is where you'll find the castle where Richard the Lion Heart was kept prisoner in 1193.

Your next stop will be at Krem. This gorgeous town

will welcome you with charming cobbled walkways in its center. This is where the newly restored Benedictine Abbey is located. This magnificent structure was built as a monastery for monks 900 years ago. The edifice was ruined by fire, plague and war yet was restored back to its glory and grandeur in the 18th century. Today, it beams proudly over the Danube Valley.

This Danube Valley trip is certainly a nice way to end a 3-day trip to Vienna. As you cruise back to the city, you can immerse yourselves in the sights, sounds, feel and taste of this magical trip.

What: Day trip through the Wachau Valley

Where: From Melk to Krems

Directions: Take a train from Vienna to Melk, tour the town and make your leisurely way by boat to Krems, 24 miles away. From Krems, take the train back to Vienna

When: Any day of the week

How Much: You can buy a combination rail/boat ticket (Vienna-Melk-Krems-Vienna) at any rail station, for about €50 depending on time/day of travel

Suggested arrival time & duration: Start your day at 9 am and you should be back by 6 pm.

8 VIENNESE CUISINE

Vienna may be a phenomenal destination for lovers of architecture, art and history, but food aficionados will also find plenty to rave about. With rich infusions of both German and Hungarian cuisines, Austrian fare is quite unlike anything you'll find in Europe. With rich, decadent desserts at the top of the list, Viennese cuisine will delight your taste buds with every mouthful.

If you love intensely flavored, hearty meals then Vienna will be your dream come true! This is the ideal destination for carnivores, sugar addicts, and anyone who prefers their food loud and proud. In Austrian cuisine, there is no room for shrinking violets, or anyone seeking to 'watch their figure'. Luckily, the city also offers plenty of walking trails to burn off the excess calories. So explore, feast…and enjoy!

Here are just some of the delectable local treats you ought to savor whilst in Vienna.

SAVOURY

Wiener Schnitzel (Viennese Schnitzel) – Known as the national dish of Austria, the world-famous schnitzel is a breaded and fried piece of veal or pork, served with potatoes or French fries: a simple but filling and memorable meal. As many would say: you've never really had a real schnitzel, until you've had a Viennese Schnitzel!

Gulash – The Hungarian national dish, a meat and vegetable stew, has infused itself in Austrian cooking over the last hundred years or so. Yet the Austrian version can be said to be even tastier, considering Austrians don't seem to share the paprika-obsession of their neighbors, so the stew has a much sweeter taste here in Vienna.

Schweinsbraten – If you've ever been to Germany you'll acquainted with the pork-obsession in this part of the world. Vienna is no different. Although not quite as fanatical about 'schwein', you'll nonetheless find this roasted pork loin dish served in all local restaurants, usually with a side dish of sauerkraut (the famed pickled cabbage) and bread dumplings.

Tafelspitz – Austrians like their beef, especially when it's simmered in a spiced broth for hours and combined with chive-horseradish sauce and side-serve of roast potatoes. The most delicious 'boiled meat' you'll ever have! If you're feeling at tad guilty at the calorie overload during your vacation, then opt for this, slightly lighter treat.

Kartoffelknödel – Large potato dumplings usually

served as accompaniment to meat dishes. As they are often served with abundant gravy, the boiled dumplings are ideal to soak up those mouthwatering sauces.

Salon Beuschel – If you lean towards the daring side of gourmet food, then this dish, made of veal lungs, heart, peppercorns, onions, capers, garlic, anchovies, and sour cream, will be just the dish for you.

Viennese Potato Soup – A thick, creamy concoction of potatoes, beef stock, mushrooms, bacon, onions, carrots, bay leaves, chives, and white wine, this soup will satisfy anyone craving for a warm and filling meal.

Stuffed Veal Kidney Roast – If you like veal, then you're in for a treat with this rich dish. It's a combination of veal loin roast stuffed with diced veal kidneys, mushrooms and spinach, and doused with a generous portion of a creamy tomato sauce. Usually served with rice or potatoes tossed with basil or parsley.

SWEET

Apfel Strudel (Apple Strudel) – Many neighboring cuisine have 'stolen' this recipe, but the original is still the best. This layered pastry is stuffed with a spiced apple filling and sprinkled with sugar. This is the most exported dessert to have come out of Austria, and makes for a delicious end to any meal and a great mid-afternoon treat.

Sachertorte (Sacher's Cake) – Another great Viennese dessert, this chocolate cake meringue has layers of apricot jam and is topped with a chocolate icing. Arguably one of the most chocolatey-chocolate cakes you'll ever taste, and the best by far! It is usually served with whipping cream on the side. Combine this with a delicious cup of coffee, and you're in heaven. Try a slice at the original home of Sachertorte, the Hotel Sacher, the most famous café in Vienna. http://www.sacher.com/

Kaiserschmarrn – A hybrid between a thin omelet and a pancake, Kaiserschmarrn is a mouth-watering delicacy and ideal for anyone who finds the desserts in Vienna a little too sweet. Mostly, because the pancake is served with its toppings (syrup, compote or jam) served on the side, so you can control the level of sweetness. Add just a tad of syrup and you'll have a fluffy Viennese version of French toast. Delish!

Knödel - The 'dumpling' is an institution in Austrian cuisine and can be found both in savory (made with bread, flour or semolina) and sweet versions, the latter made with mashed potatoes. This last mix may sound a little eccentric but trust us that, somehow, it really works! Look out for Zwetschkenknödel, a particularly delicious dumpling made with mashed potatoes, wrapped around a whole apricot, boiled and rolled in cinnamon sugar.

Topfenkolatschen – This delectable 'cheesecake' is a Moorish mix of pastry and cake. The square-shaped dessert is made of puff pastry and filled with a heavenly concoction of soft cheese, raisins, eggs and caster. You can find this sold in bakeries all over Vienna.

DRINKS

Wine – To all those who have never visited Vienna before, and are not aware of how the city is literally framed by vineyards on all sides, learning that Austrian wine is THE BOMB may come as a total surprise. Vines have been planted here for centuries and although good drops are found all over the country, Vienna is still the best place to savor them. "**Heuriger**" is the name given to traditional taverns and also the name of the current year's wine, so you'll find not only on restaurant menus but restaurant names as well. Red wine lovers ought to look out for **Zweigelt** and white wine lovers for **Gruner Veltliner** (perfectly refreshing in summer), **Schilcher** and **Welschriesling**.

Beer - A true Viennese institution, famous types are **Ottakringer Helles** and **Radler**, a refreshing and light mix of beer and sweet lemonade. If you like your beer cloudy and unfiltered then opt for a **Zwichelbeer**, or try a **Bock** if looking for a lighter version.

(Insider's Tip: if you wish to experience something totally unique and inexpensive, then head to Tongues Café, one of the latest and trendiest addition to the Viennese foodie scene. Spurred by a love of organic produce and an utter dislike of food

wastage, the guys at Tongues cook up super inexpensive vegetarian meals every day and, when all the food is gone, they close up shop. No waste, no left-overs, no excesses! If you feel like saving some bucks AND having a delicious meal, then head here at about midday)

http://www.tongues.at/

Best Cooking Classes & Food Tours in Vienna

Fallen in love with Austrian cuisine? Who could blame you!

There are a few fantastic cooking classes and tours you can join, if you have a little more time in Vienna. Because we all know that, at the end of the day, half the fun of travel is food!!

Vienna Cooking Tours & Classes - The Vienna Cooking Tours of Andrea Beck also start with a tour of the Naschmarkt. Once all the ingredients have been bought, a typical Viennese menu is cooked in the kitchen of the Gegenbauer vinegar brewery. The tours and cookery courses are offered in German, English, French and Spanish. They can be combined with a tour of the vinegar brewery.

http://www.viennacookingtours.at/

Vienna Food Walk – Funnily enough, many people wait until their second or third visit to Vienna, to make time to join a food tour, although nothing could better introduce to the city's culinary world, than doing this on your first ever day in the city.

With Vienna Food Walk, you'll spend about three hours discovering the hidden gastronomic treasures of the 1st District, and savor five local specialties and plenty of drinks. All included!

http://viennafoodwalk.at/

9 DINING IN VIENNA

Viennese love to eat! This is quite evident with the numerous coffee shops, outdoor and indoor restaurants that line every sidewalk of every street in the city. The choices will range from fine dining to casual and laid-back, to affordable and scrumptious street side cafes. You'll find plenty of traditional diners serving local specialties, and quite a few ethnic eateries to provide some variety if you wish. Either way, finding a bite to eat in this city is never going to be difficult, but if you're looking for guidance, to discover a few special places, then let us assist you.

Following are some of the most recommended restaurants in town. Prices are estimated on a dinner for two with a glass of wine.

Le Ciel – Austrian fare with a French touch

This is one of Vienna's top rated restaurants, and rightly so. The food, a fusion of Austrian and French, and service are both exquisite, and the regal ambience simply ideal for a special meal out in Vienna.

Location: Kärntner Ring 9, DISTRICT 1

Price: €120 with wine

http://www.leciel.at/

Café Imperial Wien – For a decadent coffee and cake break

This is the place to come to if you wish to try the Imperial Torte, often described as 'even better' than Sachertorte, if that's at all possible! Great coffee house, gorgeous interiors and a grand atmosphere, you'll find this café in the famed Hotel Imperial.

Location: Kärntner Ring 16, DISTRICT 1

Price: €100 on a dinner for two, but cake and coffee only €10.

http://www.cafe-imperial.at/de/

Steirereck – Fine dining in Stadtpark

This name has been synonymous to fine dining in Vienna for almost half a century. This restaurant is located in Stadtpark, on the banks of the Danube River, and enjoys a stellar outdoor eating area. Dine a la carte or choose from the 6 or 7-course degustation meals. A visit here is worthwhile…for the bread and cheese trolley alone.

Location: Am Heumarkt 2A, DISTRICT 3

Price: €210 for the 7 course degustation meal

http://steirereck.at/

Trattoria Toscana La No – A superb fix for those pasta & pizza cravings

Craving Italian whilst in Vienna? Then this is where you need to head to. This cozy little trattoria serves great handmade pasta and fantastic pizzas, as well as seafood and mouthwatering Florentine specialties.

Location: Dorotheergasse 19, DISTRICT 1

Price: €80

https://www.facebook.com/trattorialano

Café Drechsler – For a cheap and tasty meal

If you're looking for a much more affordable meal out, yet don't wish to compromise on quality of food, then check out Drechsler. Lunch deals for €7,90 per person and main courses for about €10.

Location: Linke Wienzeile 22, DISTRICT 6

Price: €20 for a lunch special for two, plus wine

http://www.cafedrechsler.at/en/home.php

TIAN – Perfect for vegetarians

Ignited by their passion for healthy living, owners of this place concocted delicious vegetarian meals which are sure to satisfy your discriminating taste buds without costing a fortune. This is one of the city's most affordable fine dining restaurants.

Location: Himmelpfortgasse 23, DISTRICT 1

Price: €89 for a 4-course set menu

http://www.taste-tian.com/restaurant/at/wien/

(Insider's Tip: some of the best meals in Vienna are enjoyed on the sidewalk! The city is home to a plethora of incredible food stalls, selling everything from traditional hot dogs, to fancy sandwiches and a myriad of pastries. Moreover, the most affordable eateries are found next to the city's main markets)

10 VIENNA BY NIGHT

Vienna may not be renowned as the most vibrant party-animal by night yet the Austrian capital does offer quite a variation of nighttime pursuits to suit everyone. From cool and trendy nightclubs, to elegant wine bars and a cultural calendar to embarrass most other capitals, there's certainly plenty here to see and do after sunset.

Here are just some of the amazing things you can in Vienna on your evenings in town.

Ride the Ferris wheel at the Prater Amusement Park

In spring and summer the Prater Amusement Park closes at midnight, so take a stroll after dinner and enjoy a sunset ride on the gigantic Ferris wheel. At the highest point, you'll be more than 200 feet off the ground an can enjoy fantastic city views.

Bar hop in the 1st District

The Jewish Quarter of the 1st District, known as the Bermuda Triangle, is awash with trendy little bars ideal for a nightcap, or two. Head here for a sociable and relaxed evening out. For a comprehensive list of the latest bars, check out this handy website: http://www.bestbarseurope.com/vienna/bars.htm

Fancy a splurge? Then head up to SKY and let the views, and cocktails, take you on a head spinning ride. http://www.skybox.at/

Enjoy a performance at the State Opera House

This is probably the most popular way for foreign visitors to experience a fantastic night out in Vienna. The Vienna Opera House hosts plenty of concerts regularly, and catching a performance at this historic venue is utterly unmissable.

Take in a bit of Jazz

After a lovely dinner, head to Jazzland and chillax with a delicious rink and some super cool tunes. Conveniently located in the heart of the 1st District, Jazzland is the idea live-music venue for foreign visitors who wish to not venture too far of an evening.

http://www.jazzland.at/

Have an Irish night out

Irish Pubs are insanely popular all over mainland Europe, and Vienna is no exception. If you fancy a pint of Guinness and a good old' chat in English, then head to the Bockshorn Irish Pub and you'll feel right at home. http://www.bockshorn.at/

Tour Vienna by Night

If you haven't had enough of the sightseeing, or even if you have, you should really join one of the many superb night tours. Seeing Vienna under the moonlight is absolutely spectacular and something you really shouldn't miss experiencing. ViennaCityTours offer a great night tour which includes a bus ride, ride on the Ferris wheel and visit to a traditional wine tavern. Perfect.

http://viennacitytours.rezgo.com/details/3179/VIENNA-BY-NIGHT

11 ACCOMMODATION

Vienna may be a relatively expensive city to visit, yet accommodation, much like food, comes in all sorts of price brackets, so even if you're on a tight budget, we can assure you, you'll find the right place to lay your head. Most of the luxe hotels are located along Ringstrasse, the major boulevard in the city.

For ease of reference, note the following price range, based on dual occupancy of a double room outside of peak travel and holiday times.

$ Budget: Less than €100

$$ Midrange: Between €100 and €200 a night

$$$ Splurge: From €200 to sky's-the-limit

Budget

Time Out City Hotel Vienna

In the very vibrant 6th district, you'll find this pleasant hotel, with minimalist décor in a lovely Art

Nouveau building. Satellite TV, WiFi and private ensuite available.

Location: Windmühlgasse 6, DISTRICT 6

Price: €40

http://www.timeout.co.at/

Do Step Inn

If the cute name doesn't appeal to you then the comfort, amenities and great location of this place certainly will. Right across the road from the western train terminal (Wien Westbahnhoff), this INN is also just a 5-minute walk away from the major shopping street: Mariahilferstrasse.

Location: Felberstraße 20, DISTRICT 15

Price: €40

http://www.dostepinn.com/

Vienna Hostel Ruthensteiner

An independent backpacker hostel in a homey atmosphere, the Ruthensteiner is a stone's throw away from Palace Schönbrunn and the city center. Located on a quiet street, this place is ideal for individual travelers or small family groups travelling on a budget.

Location: Robert Hamerlinggasse 24, DISTRICT 15

Price: €55

http://www.hostelruthensteiner.com/

(Insider's Tip: as with most European cities, the most affordable accommodation choices are near the Central Railway Station (Hauptbahnhof) so if you're looking to spend even less than our 'Budget' recommendations, you'd do well to search in that area. Moreover, most of the cheaper options lack an English version to their websites, so simply Google their name and you can view the page in Goggle Translate)

Midrange

Austria Trend Hotel Europa Wien

This hotel is located near the major tourist attractions in Vienna. Complete with amenities and facilities, it has 160 guestrooms and bar/lounge.

Location: Kaerntnerstrasse 18, DISTRICT 1

Price: €100

http://www.austria-trend.at/Hotel-Europa-Wien/en/

Pension Suzanne

Pension Suzanne, a family run boutique guesthouse, is also a great alternative with its superb service and unbeatable central location.

Location: Walfischgasse 4, DISTRICT 1

Price: €120

http://www.pension-suzanne.at/index.en.php

Hotel Altstadt Vienna

You may also want to check out the Altstadt, which is just outside the Ring and offers a great mix of styles from classic to avant-garde.

Location: Kirchengasse 41, DISTRICT 7

Price: €150

http://www.altstadt.at/

Hotel Kaiserin Elisabeth

This is a hotel with a turn-of-the-century touch. It has beautifully appointed rooms and friendly staff. Very accessible as it is located near the main sights of central Vienna including St. Stephen's Cathedral, the Vienna State Opera and many more.

Location: Weihburggasse 3, DISTRICT 1

Price: €160

http://www.kaiserinelisabeth.at/en/

Hotel Karntnerhof

This is a boutique hotel with a timeless design located in a 19th-century building. It offers personalized service, stylish rooms, and complete amenities. Rich in its own history, this hotel is called Vienna's smallest Grand Hotel.

Location: Grashofgasse 4

Price: €180

http://www.karntnerhof.com/english/

Splurge

Grand Hotel Wien

The Grand Hotel is a stylish and classy Viennese hub which has been around since the early 20th century but has retained its elegance and grandeur. The Grand Hotel caters to those of exquisite tastes, budget and standards in style.

Location: Kartner Ring 9, DISTRICT 1

Price: €340

http://www.grandhotelwien.at/

Hotel Imperial

This is a 5-star hotel combining a traditional décor with modern amenities. Hotel Imperial is often dubbed as the grand old dame of Vienna. Built in 1873, this is one of the most luxurious hotels in the city and part of the Starwood Hotel Group.

Location: Kaemtner Ring 16, DDISTRICT 1

Price: €830

http://www.imperialvienna.com/

Palais Coburg Residenz

This luxurious hotel serves as the official residence for visiting royalties from Britain, France, Hungary, Portugal, Bulgaria and many more. This place boasts of sophistication, class, ultimate style, outstanding architecture and world-class service and amenities…when nothing but the best will do.

Location: Coburgbastei 4, DISTRICT 1

Price: €900

http://palais-coburg.com/en/

12 OTHER RECOMMENDED PLACES TO VISIT

MQ Museums Quartier

This is an art center near the Imperial Palace, which boasts of prominent museums and art galleries. It also has a bustling café and restaurant scene where you can enjoy good food and drinks after museum-hopping.

Volksprater/Wurechtelprater

An amusement park in Vienna which offers a lot of fun activities which include carnival games, ghost trains, rollercoasters, and the Prater, an 110-year old, 64.75 meter high Ferris wheel. When you reach the highest point of this ride, you'll enjoy a magnificent view of the city.

Freihausviertel

Very near Naschmarkt, this place has become the converging point of the city's contemporary art scene. Galleries, antique shops, fashion designers, and flower shops line up the streets providing a fusion of art, culture and history. There is also a mix of bars, cafés and restaurants in this area.

Vienna's Christmas Markets

During the winter months of November and December each year, the squares and streets of Vienna come alive with the splendor of bright colors and glistening lights ushering in the merriest festivities. The whole city becomes magical, paying tribute to an age-old tradition. The Yuletide Season is welcomed with quite a number of markets in the city selling a wide variety of goods. Savor the aroma of freshly-made candied fruits, hot chestnuts, the best pastries and bread wafting through the air. They have a lot of activities lined up for everyone and most especially the kids. It is the season to be merry and nowhere else can one feel the best of the Christmas spirit but in the city of Vienna.

13 GERMAN LANGUAGE ESSENTIALS

English speakers will find little issue in communicating with the locals of Berlin. However, if you want to learn some of their essential phrases for directions, a restaurant or a hotel, here is a list to prepare you for your trip to Vienna.

Greetings:

Good day

Guten Tag.

(*GOO-ten tahk*)

Goodbye

Auf Wiedersehen.

(*owf VEE-dur-zane*)

Good morning

Guten Morgen

(*GOO-tun MOR-gun*)

Good evening

Guten Abend

(*GOO-tun AH-bunt*)

Good night

Schönen Abend noch.

(*shur-nun AH-bunt nokh*)

Good night (*to sleep*)

Gute Nacht.

(*GOO-tuh nakht*)

Directions:

How do I get to _____? (cities)

Wie komme ich nach _____?

(*vee KOM-muh ikh nahkh _____?*)

How do I get to _____? (places, streets)

Wie komme ich zum/zur _____?

(*vee KOM-muh ikh tsoom/tsoor _____?*)

...the train station?

...zum Bahnhof?

(*tsoom BAHN-hohf?*)

...the bus station / bus stop?

.zum Busbahnhof / zur Bushaltestelle?

(*tsoom BOOSS-BAHN-hohf/tsoor BOOSS-hahl-tuh-shteh-luh?*)

...the airport?

...zum Flughafen?

(*tsoom FLOOG-hah-fen?*)

...downtown?

...zur Stadtmitte?

(*tsoor SHTUT-mit-tuh*)

...the youth hostel?

...zur Jugendherberge?

(*tsoor YOO-gent-hayr-bayr-guh*)

...the _____ hotel?

...zum _____ Hotel?

(*tsoom _____ hoh-TELL*)

...the American/Canadian/Australian/British consulate?

...zum amerikanischen/kanadischen/australischen/britischen Konsulat?

(*tsoom ah-mayr-ih-KAHN-ish-en/kah-NAH-dish-en/ous-TRAH-lish-en/BRIT-ish-en kon-zoo-LAHT?*)

Where are there a lot of...

Wo gibt es viele... (?)

(*VOU gipt ess FEE-luh...*)

...hotels?

...Hotels?

(*hoh-TELLSS*)

...restaurants?

...Restaurants?

(*rest-oh-RAHNTS?*)

...sites to see?

...Sehenswürdigkeiten?

(*ZAY-ens-vuur-dikh-kigh-ten?*)

Can you show me on the map?

Kannst du/Können Sie mir das auf der Karte zeigen?

(*kahnst doo/KOON-en zee meer dahss ouf dayr KAHR-tuh TSIGH-gen?*)

street, road

Straße

(*SHTRAH-suh*)

Left

links

(*links*)

Right

rechts

(*rekhts*)

Turn left

Links abbiegen.

(*LINKS AHP-bee-gen*)

Turn right

Rechts abbiegen

(*REKHTS AHP-bee-gen*)

straight ahead

geradeaus

(*guh-RAH-duh-OWSS*)

At the Restaurant:

A table for one person/two people, please.

Ein Tisch für eine Person/zwei Personen, bitte.

(*ighn TISH fuur IGHN-uh payr-ZOHN/TSVIGH payr-ZOHN-nen, BIT-tuh*)

Can I look at the menu, please?

Ich hätte gerne die Speisekarte.

(*ikh HET-tuh GAYR-nuh dee SHPIGH-zuh-kahr-tuh*)

Is there a house specialty?

Gibt es eine Spezialität des Hauses?

(*gipt ess igh-nuh shpeh-tsyah-lee-TAYT dess HOW-zess?*)

Is there a local specialty?

Gibt es eine Spezialität aus dieser Gegend?

(*gipt ess igh-nuh shpeh-tsyah-lee-TAYT owss DEE-zer GAY-gent?*)

I'm a vegetarian.

Ich bin Vegetarier.

(*ikh bin vay-gay-TAH-ree-er*)

I don't eat pork.

Ich esse kein Schweinefleisch.

(*ikh ESS-uh kign SHVIGN-uh-flighsh*)

I only eat kosher food.

Ich esse nur koscher.

(*ikh ESS-uh noor KOH-sher*)

At the Hotel:

Do you have any rooms available?

Sind noch Zimmer frei?

(*ZINT nokh TSIM-mer FRIGH?*)

How much is a room for one person/two people?

Wie viel kostet ein Einzelzimmer/Doppelzimmer?

(*vee-feel KOSS-tet ighn IGHN-tsel-tsim-mer/DOP-pel-tsim-mer?*)

Does the room come with...

Hat das Zimmer...

(*HAHT dahss TSIM-mer...*)

...bedsheets?

...Bettlaken?

(*...BET-lahk-en?*)

...a bathroom? (toilet)

...eine Toilette?

(*igh-nuh to-ah-LET-tuh?*)

...a telephone?

...ein Telefon?

(*ighn tell-eh-FOHN?*)

...a TV?

...einen Fernseher?

(*igh-nen FAYRN-zay-er?*)

May I see the room first?

Kann ich das Zimmer erstmal sehen?

(*kahn ikh dahs TSIM-mer ayrst-mahl ZAY-en?*)

Do you have anything quieter?

Haben Sie etwas Ruhigeres?

(*HAH-ben zee ET-vahs ROO-ig-er-ess?*)

...bigger?

...größeres?

(*GROO-ser-ess?*)

...cheaper?

...billigeres?

(*BILL-ig-er-ess?*)

OK, I'll take it.

OK, ich nehme es.

(*OH-kay, ikh NAY-muh ess*)

I will stay for _____ night(s).

Ich bleibe eine Nacht (_____ Nächte).

(*ihk BLIGH-buh IGH-nuh nahkht/_____ NEKH-tuh*) **Note:***The plural of* Nacht' *is* 'Nächte'.

Social:

How are you? (*used as a real question, not a form of greeting.*)

Wie geht's?

(*vee GATES?*)

Fine, thank you.

Gut, danke.

(*goot, DAN-keh*)

What is your name? (*formal*)

Wie heißen Sie?

(*vee HIGH-sun zee?*)

What is your name? (*informal*)

Wie heißt du?

(*vee HIGHST doo?*)

My name is _____ .

Ich heiße _____ .

(*eesh HIGH-suh*)

Nice to meet you. (formal)

Nett, Sie kennen zu lernen.

(*net zee KEN-en tsoo LER-nen*)

Nice to meet you. (informal)

Nett, dich kennen zu lernen.

(*net deesh KEN-en tsoo LER-nen*)

Please.

Bitte.

(*BEE-tuh*)

Thank you.

Danke schön.

(*DAN-kuh shurn*)

Thanks.

Danke.

(*DAN-kuh*)

You're welcome.

Bitte schön!

(*BEE-tuh shurn*)

Yes.

Ja.

(*yah*)

No.

Nein.

(*nine*)

Excuse me. (*getting attention*)

Entschuldigen Sie.

(*ent-SHOOL-dee-gun zee*)

Excuse me. (*begging pardon*)

Entschuldigung.

(*ent-SHOOL-dee-goong*)

I'm sorry.

Es tut mir leid.

(*es toot meer lite*)

I can't speak German (well).

Ich kann nicht [so gut] Deutsch sprechen.

(*eesh kahn nikht [zo goot] doytsh shprekhen*)

Do you speak English? (formal)

Sprechen Sie Englisch?

(*shprekhun zee ENG-leesh*)

Is there someone here who speaks English?

Gibt es hier jemanden, der Englisch spricht?

(*geept es heer yeh-MAHN-dun dare ENG-leesh shprikht*)

14 CONCLUSION

For three days, you have traveled to a place where dreams are made. You've seen the remnants of a majestic past, been transported back in time, to the glory of a bygone era where the grand monarchs ruled. The scenes, the action, the drama of a royal lifestyle seem to have been re-enacted before your very eyes. You were there, where it all once happened.

You've walked through dance halls where kings and the queens danced, clad in robes and gowns and donning crowns. You've watched operas, theatrical performances and musical concertos in pillared balconies. As you grew weary from it all, you've lazily lounged and taken respite under the shades of their trees, read a book, gazed at the sun and just emptied your thoughts into the horizon. You have sailed on the Danube River, seen the countryside and were overwhelmed by their steep vineyards. You savored classic Austrian foods and sipped aged wines.

When nighttime descended upon you, you

comfortably slept in their cozy rooms. This is a tale that will forever be true. Vienna will live long in your memories. It has given you not just an ordinary tour but a mind and soul-enriching experience.

Bis wir uns wiedersehen!

Printed in Great Britain
by Amazon